VOCAL SELECTIONS

FROM

THE MUSIC MAN

By
MEREDITH WILLSON

Contents

FRANK MUSIC CORP. and MEREDITH WILLSON MUSIC

Applications for performance of this work, whether legitimate, stock,
amateur, or foreign, should be addressed to:
MUSIC THEATRE INTERNATIONAL
545 Eighth Avenue
New York, NY 10018
(212)868-6668

Seventy Six Trombones

From the Musical Comedy "The Music Man"

By MEREDITH WILLSON

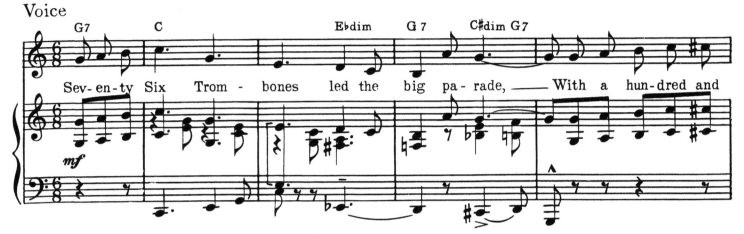

Sev-en-ty Six Trom - bones led the big pa - rade, ____ With a hun-dred and

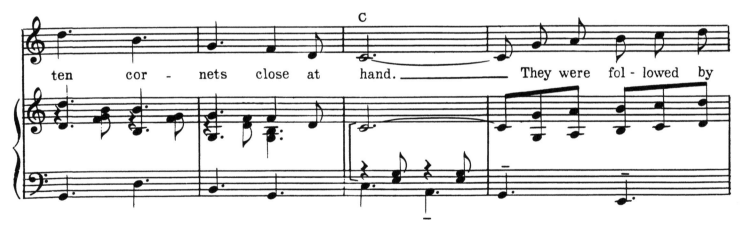

ten cor - nets close at hand. ____ They were fol - lowed by

rows and rows of the fin-est vir-tu - o - sos, The cream of

ev - 'ry fa - mous band._____ Sev - en - ty Six Trom -

bones caught the morn-ing sun,_____With a hun-dred and ten cor - nets right be-

hind._____ There were more than a thou - sand reeds spring-ing up like

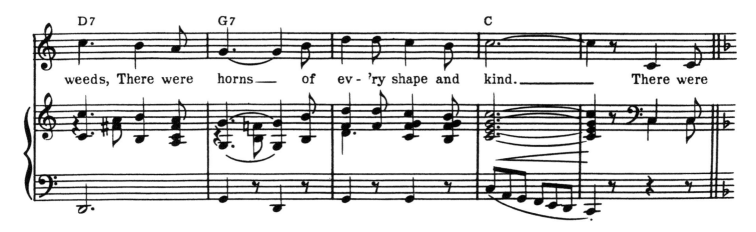

weeds, There were horns___ of ev - 'ry shape and kind._____ There were

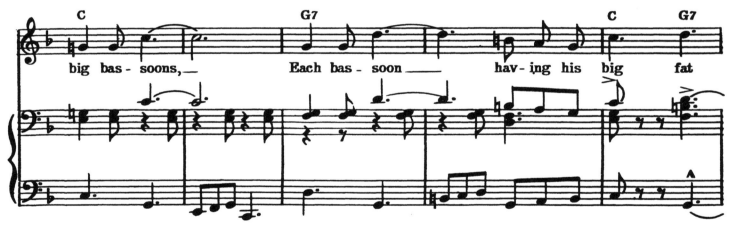

Thun - der - ing, thun - der - ing, loud - er than be - fore. Clar - i nets of

ev - 'ry size and trum - pet - ers who'd im - pro - vise a full oc - tave high - er than the

score.

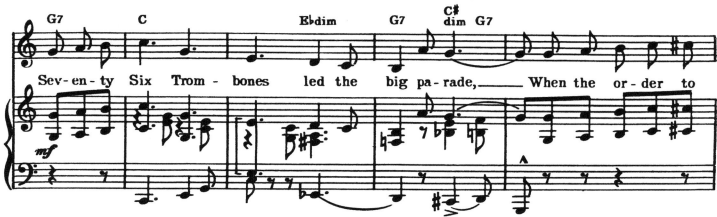

Sev - en - ty Six Trom - bones led the big pa - rade,____ When the or - der to

march rang out loud and clear._____ Start-ing off with a big bang

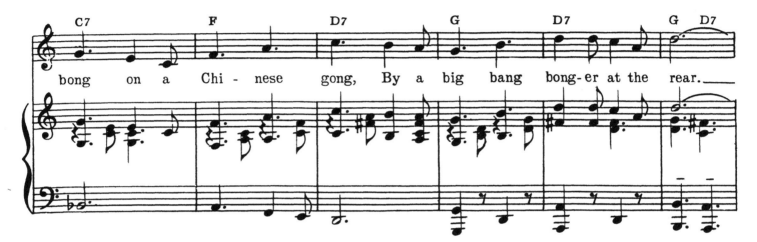

bong on a Chi - nese gong, By a big bang bong-er at the rear._____

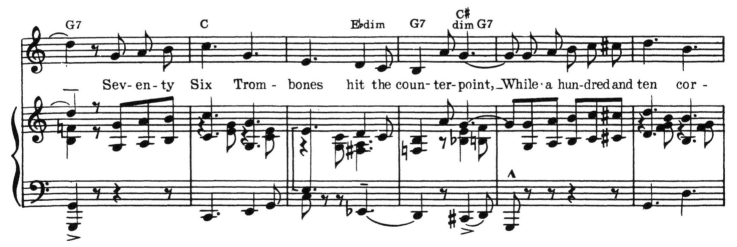

Sev-en-ty Six Trom - bones hit the coun-ter-point,_While·a hun-dred and ten cor -

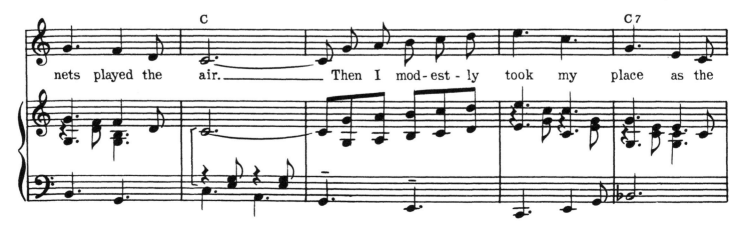

nets played the air._____ Then I mod-est-ly took my place as the

one and on-ly bass, And I oom-pahed up and down the square.____

A la Tuba

Buh buh buh buh buh buh buh buh buh buh buh,____ Buh buh buh buh buh

buh buh buh buh buh buh.____ Buh buh buh buh buh

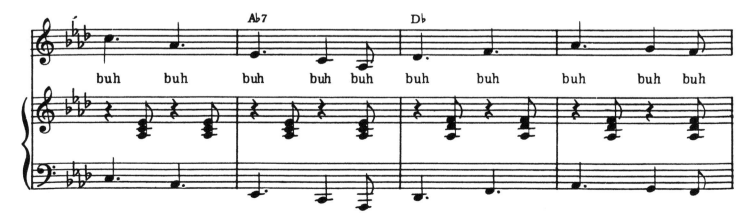

buh buh buh buh buh buh buh buh buh buh

buh _____ buh buh buh buh buh buh. _____

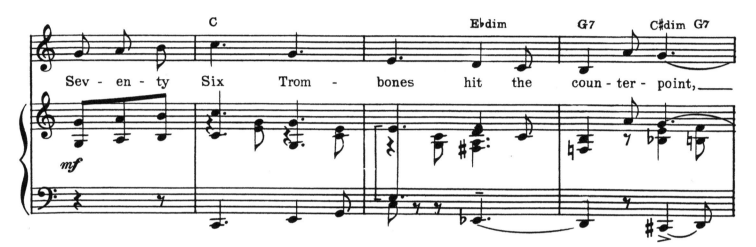

Sev - en - ty Six Trom - bones hit the coun - ter - point, ____

____ While a hun - dred and ten cor - nets played the air. ____

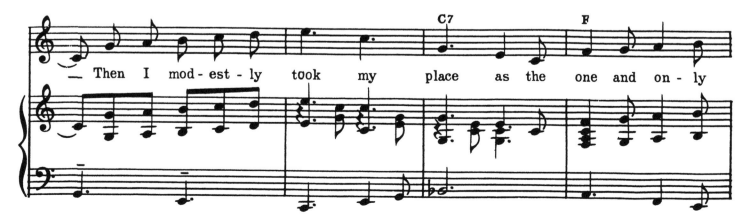

____ Then I mod - est - ly took my place as the one and on - ly

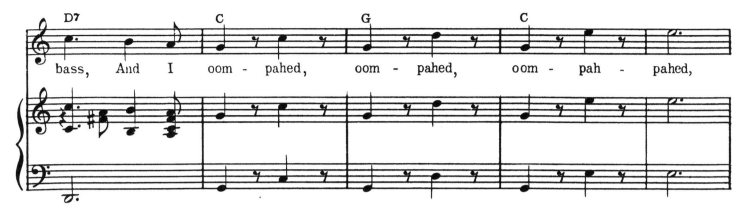

bass, And I oom - pahed, oom - pahed, oom - pah - pahed,

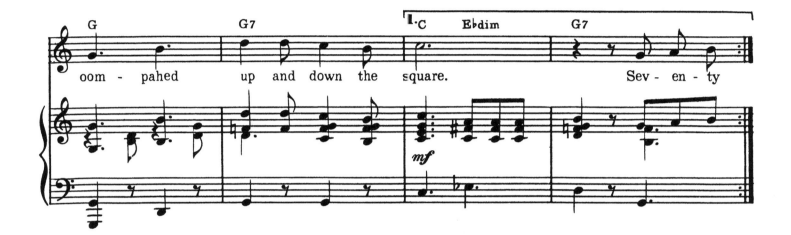

oom - pahed up and down the square. Sev - en - ty

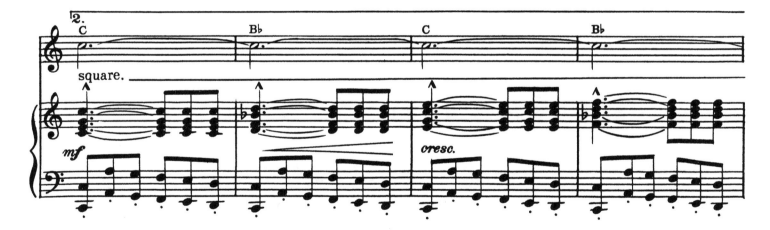

square.

It's You

From the Musical Comedy "The Music Man"

By MEREDITH WILLSON

It's You in the sun-rise, It's You in my cup, It's

You all the way in-to town. _____ It's your sweet "hel-lo,

_dear," that sets me up, It's your "got to go, ____ dear" that

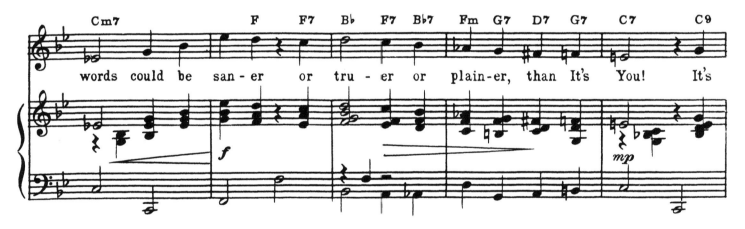

My White Knight

From the Musical Comedy "The Music Man"

By
MEREDITH WILLSON

Moderato

Piano

Voice

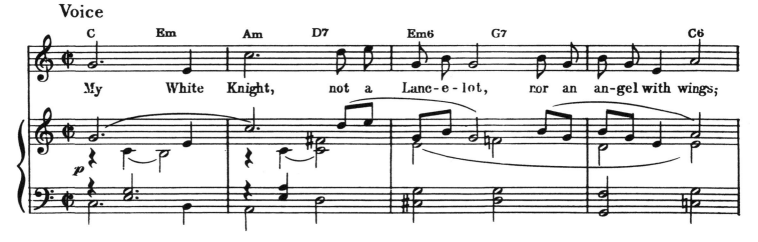

My White Knight, not a Lanc-e-lot, nor an an-gel with wings;

Just some-one to love me, who is not a-shamed of a few nice things.

My White Knight, what my heart would say if it on-ly knew how. Please, dear

Ve - nus, show me now. All I want is a plain man;

All I want is a mod - est man; A qui - et man, a gen - tle man, A straight-for-ward and

hon - est man to sit with me in a cot-tage some-where in the state of I - o - wa.

— And I would like him to be_____ more in-t'rest-ed in me_____

than he is in him-self. And more in-t'rest-ed in us than in me.

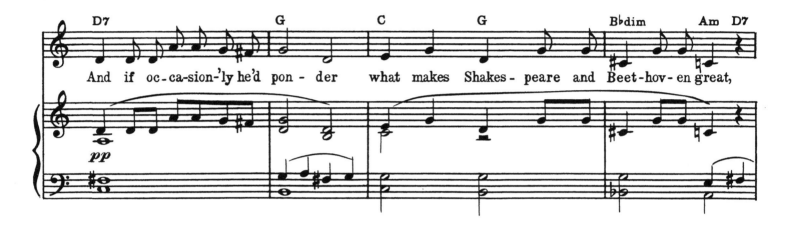

And if oc-ca-sion-'ly he'd pon - der what makes Shakes-peare and Beet-hov-en great,

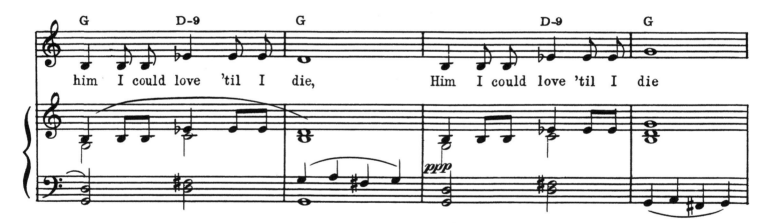

him I could love 'til I die, Him I could love 'til I die

My White Knight, not a Lanc-e-lot, nor an an-gel with wings

Just some-one to love me, who is not a-shamed of a few nice things.

My White Knight, let me walk with him where the oth-ers ride by;

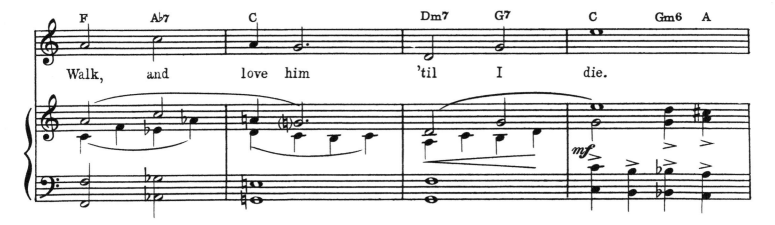

Walk, and love him 'til I die.

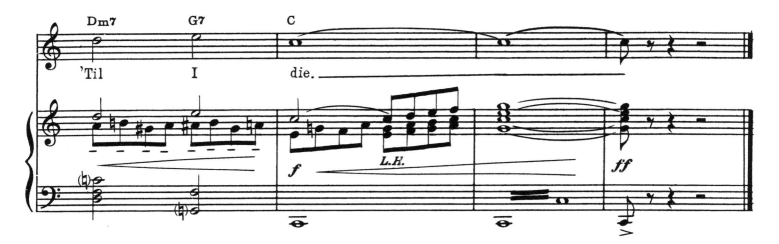

'Til I die._____

Lida Rose

From the Musical Comedy "The Music Man"

By MEREDITH WILLSON

thou - sand kiss - es shy. Ding, dong, ding! I can

hear the chap-el bell chime. Ding, dong, ding! At the

least sug-ges-tion I'll pop the ques-tion. Li - da Rose, I'm

home a - gain, Rose,_ with - out a sweet-heart to my name.

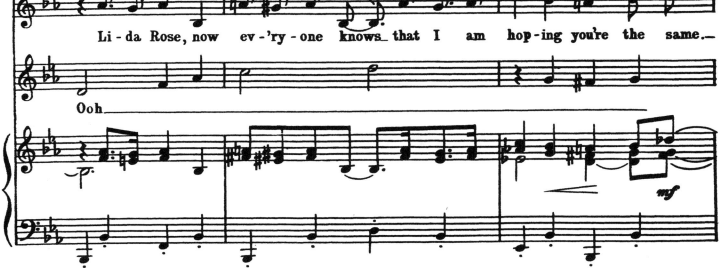

Li - da Rose, now ev - 'ry-one knows_ that I am hop-ing you're the same._

So here is my love song, Not fan - cy or

Till There Was You

From the Musical Comedy "The Music Man"

By MEREDITH WILLSON

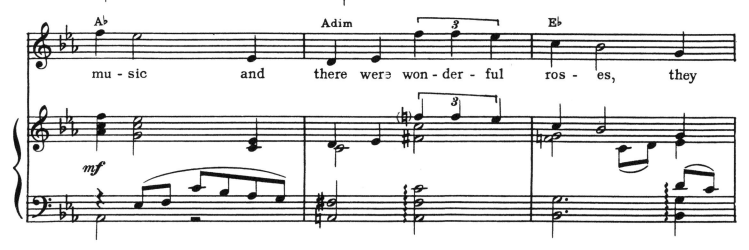

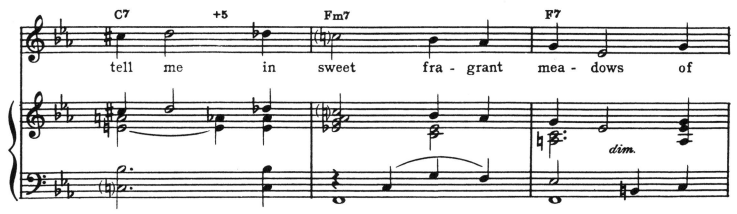

dawn, and dew, There was love all a-

round, but I nev-er heard it sing-ing, No, I

nev-er heard it at all Till There Was You.

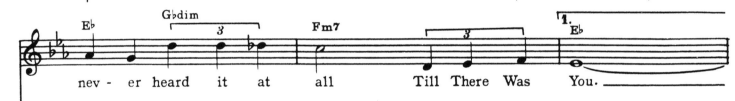

There were You.

The Wells Fargo Wagon

From the Musical Comedy "The Music Man"

By
MEREDITH WILLSON

Wells Far - go Wag - on is a - com - in' down the street, I wish, I wish I knew what it could
Wells Far - go Wag - on is a - com - in' down the street, I wish I knew what he was com - in'

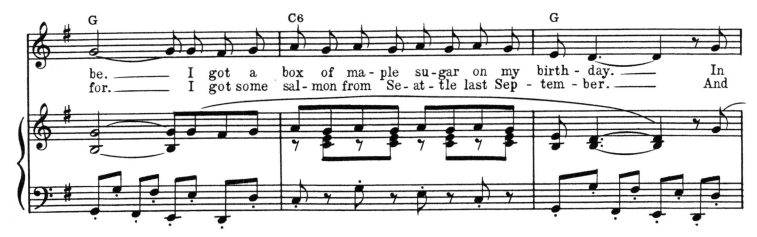

be. ___ I got a box of ma - ple su - gar on my birth - day. ___ In
for. ___ I got some sal - mon from Se - at - tle last Sep - tem - ber. ___ And

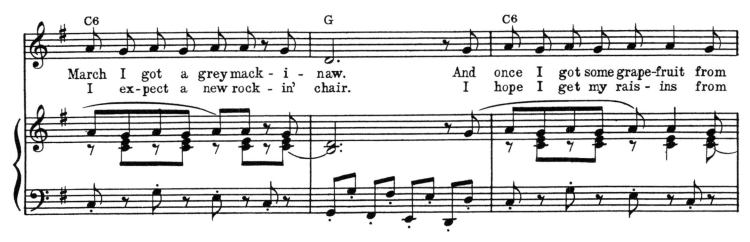

March I got a grey mack - i - naw. And once I got some grape-fruit from
I ex - pect a new rock - in' chair. I hope I get my rais - ins from

Tam - pa. ___ Mont-gom - 'ry Ward sent me a bath-tub and a cross-cut saw. O-ho, the
Fres - no. ___ The D. A. R. have sent a can-non for the court-house square. O-ho, the

Wells Far-go Wag-on is a - com-in' now. Is it a pre-paid sur-prise or C. O.
Wells Far-go Wag-on is a - com-in' now, I don't know how I can ev-er wait to

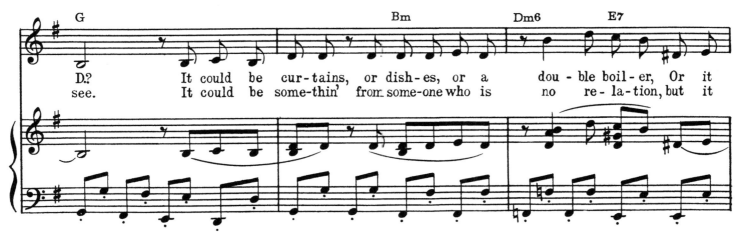

D.? It could be cur-tains, or dish-es, or a dou-ble boil-er, Or it
see. It could be some-thin' from some-one who is no re-la-tion, but it

could be _____ some-thin' spe-cial just for me. _____
could be _____ some-thin' spe-cial just for

O - ho the me. _____

Goodnight, My Someone

From the Musical Comedy "The Music Man"

By MEREDITH WILLSON

yours, dear, if dreams there be; Sweet dreams to car-ry you close to

me. I wish they may and I wish they might. Now Good-night, My

Some-one, Good - night. Good - night. good -

night, good - night, good - night.

Gary, Indiana

From the Musical Comedy "The Music Man"

By
MEREDITH WILLSON

an - a, that's the town that knew me when. If you'd

like to have a log-i-cal ex-pla - na - tion___ how I

hap-pened on this el-e-gant syn - co - pa - tion,___ I will

say with-out a mo-ment of hes - i - ta - tion,___ There is

just one place that can light my face Ga - ry, In - di - an - a, Ga - ry,

In - di - an - a, Not Lou-is - i - an - a, Par - is, France, New York or Rome, but

Ga - ry, In - di - an - a, Ga - ry, In - di - an - a, Ga - ry, In - di - an - a, my home sweet

home.   If you'd   home. _____